TANK:
The M1A1 Abrams

Michael A. Black

HIGH
interest
books

Children's Press

New   hing / Sydney

To my father, Andrew F. Black

Book Design: MaryJane Wojciechowski
Contributing Editor: Mark Beyer

Photo Credits: Cover, pp. 9, 10, 13, 18, 21, 35, 39 © Photri Inc; p. 5 © Edimedia/Corbis; p. 6 © Bettman/Corbis; p. 14 © Reuters/Archive Photos; p. 16 © Yves Debay; The Military Picture Library/Corbis; p. 25 © Department of Defense/Sgt. Oscar Martinez, U.S. Marine Corps.; p. 27 © Department of Defense; p. 28 Mark Gibson/Index Stock; p. 31 © Department of Defense/Lance Cpl. S. A. Harwood, U.S. Marine Corps.; p. 32 © Underwood & Underwood/Corbis; p. 33 © Department of Defense/Spc. Sharron Grey, U.S. Army; p. 36 © Peter Turnley/Corbis: p. 40 © Department of Defense/Lance Cpl. W. Makela, U.S. Marine Corps.; p. 40a Department of Defense/Lance Cpl. Michelle L. Underwood, U.S. Marine Corps.; p. 40b © Department of Defense/Staff Sgt. Chris Steffen, U.S. Air Force

Visit Children's Press on the Internet at:
http://publishing.grolier.com

Library of Congress Cataloging-in-Publication Data

Black, Michael A., 1949-
 Tanks : the M1A1 Abrams / by Michael A. Black.
  p. cm. – (High-tech military weapons)
 Includes bibliographical references and index.
 Summary: Provides general information about tanks and specific facts
  about the features and operation of the M1A1 Abrams tank.
 ISBN 0-516-23342-4 (lib. bdg.) – ISBN 0-516-23542-7 (pbk.)
 1. M1 (Tank)—Juvenile literature. [1. M1 (Tank) 2. Tanks (Military
 science)] I. Title. II. Series.

UG446.5 .B5745 2000
623.7'4752—dc21

00-027944

CONTENTS

INTRODUCTION

The idea for using an armored vehicle for protection in battle dates from the 1500s. The famous painter and inventor Leonardo da Vinci designed such vehicles. However, the first use of what we know as "tanks" was in 1917 during World War I (1914–1918). The main battlefield during this war was made up of long lines of ditches or trenches. Men and weapons filled these ditches. They lived in them, fought in them, and died in them. A British general used an armored vehicle with treads to break through the barbed wire and machine-gun positions of the enemy lines. Tank warfare began. Tanks quickly became the most fearsome weapon in war. For the rest of the twentieth century, tank design changed and improved. Today, experts call the M1A1 Abrams the best tank in the world.

Leonardo da Vinci drew pictures of armored vehicles
four hundred years before engines were invented.

CHAPTER 1

THE NEED FOR TANKS

The first tanks were crude and slow-moving. The British and French used tanks during World War I to break through the long trenches dug to hide enemy troops. But the armies didn't know how to use tanks well. Tanks were used to help the foot soldiers move forward during battle. The foot soldiers hid behind the tanks as they marched toward the enemy. Once they reached the enemy, the foot soldiers did the fighting. A great chance was wasted to use the tank as a fighting vehicle.

American tanks during World War II (1939-1945) were small and slow. Their armor made them deadly.

As time passed, however, military commanders invented new ways to use tanks. The science of how to use weapons is called tactics. Military commanders began to see the tank as an offensive weapon. They wanted to use the tank to blast away at enemy buildings, trucks, and bridges. In addition to improved tactics, tank design also improved. By World War II (1939–1945), tanks were faster, had more steel armor, and more powerful cannons. These improvements made tanks the most-feared weapon on the battlefield. Tanks made up whole fighting units. The German army used large groups of tanks during its quick attacks. The Allies (England, France, the Soviet Union, the United States, and twenty-six other nations) learned these tactics too. Soon they struck back with their own tank units in time to help win the war.

After World War II, political relations between the United States and the Soviet

The Soviet Union built and used the T-72 as
its main battle tank throughout the cold war.

Union were tense. There was a possibility of
war between these two powerful countries.
These years of tension were called the cold
war (1946–1990). During this time, the
United States and the Soviet Union com-
peted to build the better tank. The result was
two high-tech tanks. The Soviet army built a
tank called the T-72. The U.S. Army built the
M1A1 Abrams. The Americans and the
Soviets never fought against each other.
However, their two tanks fought during the

Handheld rockets are dangerous to tanks
because they can be used from almost anywhere.

Gulf War (1991). The Iraqi army used the Soviet-made T-72s against the American-made M1A1 Abrams. When the smoke cleared, the Abrams tank proved that it had stronger armor and greater firepower.

BUILDING THE ABRAMS M1A1

In the early 1970s, the United States started to develop the Abrams M1A1 tank to replace the older tanks. They wanted a new tank that would be the battlefield weapon of the future. Experience in battle had shown that tanks were unprotected against handheld rocket launchers. These rocket launchers were effective weapons. They were easy to carry, and were capable of destroying a tank. Tank designers had to think of how to combat such dangerous weapons. They came up with the Abrams M1A1.

THE ABRAMS'S DESIGN

To protect the tank crew, the Abrams is designed to be flatter and lower to the ground than are older tanks. The Abrams is flat because its body and turret (the rotating part that sits on top of the body of the tank) are built at angles to the ground. Only the sides of the tank are built straight up and down. These angled surfaces allowed the designers to build a larger tank that is safer for the crew. Having these angles helps the tank to deflect enemy fire. If a bullet hits an upright flat surface, it can go through it. If the surface is at an angle, the bullet skips off the surface.

The Abrams's flatness makes it lower to the ground. Being lower to the ground makes the Abrams harder to hit. This is because its profile is shorter than those of older tanks. A short tank is a smaller target. Smaller targets are harder to hit.

The Abrams's turret is specially made. It has panels that blow upward when struck by incoming shells. This action takes away much of the force that the shell normally would have. The space between these panels leaves the inside of the tank unharmed.

Another change from the older tanks is the Abrams's engine. Older tanks had diesel (a type of gasoline) engines. Not only were the diesel engines noisy, they were slow as well. The Abrams runs on regular gasoline. Regular gasoline is used in engines built for speed.

Big engines help tanks to
move fast over almost any terrain.

The Abrams is the first tank to use a turbine engine. Turbine engines also are used on jet planes. The Abrams can go as fast as 50 miles per hour on flat surfaces such as an open road. This top speed is very fast when you consider that the Abrams weighs more than 54 tons. That's as heavy as 50 automobiles! The Abrams's powerful engine can accelerate to 20 miles per hour in only 6 seconds. And it can go 300 miles on a single tank of gas.

CHAPTER 2

THE ABRAMS CREW AND ARMAMENTS

The M1A1 Abrams has a crew of four soldiers. There is the commander, the gunner, the loader, and the driver. Each crew member has at least one job. The crew uses a variety of devices and weapons to help them find and destroy the enemy.

The commander, loader, and gunner sit in the turret section of the Abrams tank. This is the largest area inside the tank. The turret contains the tank's main gun. This gun is a long cannon. It shoots 105-millimeter shells. The shells can hit a target more than 2 miles

The Abrams's commander, loader, and gunner sit in the turret. The driver sits at the front of the tank.

The M1A1 Abrams carries two machine
guns and a smoke-grenade launcher.

away. On top of the turret there are also two
machine guns and a smoke-grenade launcher.
Smoke grenades are used to send out smoke
that hides the tanks from enemy sight during
battle.

The driver sits low in the front of the tank. He is nearly lying flat as he steers the tank. This allows the tank body to be low to the ground.

THE COMMANDER

The commander is the man who directs the tank. The other members of the crew follow his orders. In battle, the commander decides where to go, what to attack, and which type of ammunition to use. The commander sits in the right section of the turret. He has six periscopes that allow him to see in a complete circle around the M1A1.

Besides finding the enemy himself, the commander receives information about the enemy from both his gunner and his driver. They also have viewfinders to help them see outside the tank. The commander has the same firing controls as the gunner. This allows both of them to fire the main cannon and the machine gun next to it.

The Abrams crew uses different electronic devices to aim and fire their weapons.

THE GUNNER

The second member of the crew is called the gunner. He sits in front of the commander on the right side of the turret. The gunner uses computers to help him locate the enemy. Once an enemy target is found, the gunner aims the cannon. He gets his orders to fire at the target from the commander.

The gunner has a special device used to see outside the tank. This device is called a viewfinder. The viewfinder shows on a video screen what is outside the tank. This screen also uses a system that helps the gunner to see at night.

Its ability to locate the enemy at night makes the M1A1 Abrams a powerful weapon. The device that allows the gunner (and commander) to see at night is called the thermal imaging system (TIS). This system works on an object's heat. The heat an object gives off is captured by the computer. The heat (thermal) image is displayed in the gunner's eyepiece. A laser beam then shows exactly how far away the target is. This laser beam is called a rangefinder. The gunner aims the Abrams's gun at the enemy and fires it on the commander's order.

THE LOADER

The third member of the crew is the loader. The loader sits to the left of the commander in the turret. The loader chooses ammunition from a storage container and places the shell into the gun. The Abrams's ability to fire quickly often is dependent on the loader. The loader must quickly put the shell into the rear of the gun (the breach). After the gun fires, the loader must quickly release the gun breach. The breach sends the spent shell casing into the loader's waiting arms. The loader must then quickly turn and put the spent casing into its slot in a special storage container. Now he is ready to get another shell and load the gun.

The shell storage containers have plastic slots that stop the shells from bumping against each other. Heavy doors shield the crew from an explosion if the ammunition container is hit by enemy fire. The Abrams holds up to sixty rounds of ammunition.

The loader is responsible for shells that will be fired from the tank's cannon.

The Abrams has different kinds of ammunition that can be fired. The commander chooses the type of ammunition to be used. This ammunition includes armor-piercing rounds and high-explosive rounds. The armor-piercing ammunition is made from depleted uranium. Uranium is the heaviest metal on Earth. However, depleted uranium is not radioactive. The uranium shell is so heavy that it can slash through an enemy tank's armor like a knife through butter.

THE DRIVER

The driver is the fourth member of the tank crew. His position is at the front of the Abrams tank. Here he uses a handlebar control with a throttle, and foot pedals, to drive and steer the tank. He also has a control panel that shows the gas, fluid levels, battery, and electrical equipment.

The driver has three periscopes that help him to steer the tank. The periscopes allow him to see forward 120 degrees from left to right. One of the three periscopes is a central image intensifying periscope. This periscope allows the driver to see at night. Although the driver actually drives the tank, he follows the commander's directions.

CHAPTER 3

THE ABRAMS DEFENSE SYSTEMS

Today, land mines and handheld rockets are just two of the deadly weapons that can harm or destroy Abrams M1A1 tanks. Also, the threat of nuclear and chemical warfare makes the use of armored vehicles more important than ever. Tanks have to protect their crews from such things as radioactive fallout (the radiation that is released in the air following a nuclear explosion) and chemical weapons. The Abrams M1A1 has been designed to combat each threat.

LAND MINES

A land mine is a buried explosive device. It blows up when a certain amount of weight is put on it. Sometimes the weight of a soldier makes it explode. Other times a vehicle's weight can make it explode. Land mines were a problem during World War II. A specially designed attachment called the "crab" was hooked to the front of a tank. The crab was a rotating drum with chains attached. An extended metal arm held the drum several feet in front of the tank. As the drum rotated, the chain would whip around and detonate the buried mines.

During the Gulf War, large shovel-like plows were used to combat mines. They were put on the front of the first tank to go through the minefield. The long blades exploded the mines. The shovel was an added protection to the tank. Not all tanks were equipped with the plows. Only a few in each tank group had

Some Abrams tanks have a plow attached to the front
of them to push land mines out of the way.

them. Those tanks would move through an
area first to plow a clear path. The rest of the
tanks would follow in the path that the first
tank had cleared.

ROCKET LAUNCHERS

The handheld rocket launcher is exactly what
its name sounds like. A person holds a
launcher that has a rocket inside its barrel.
These handheld rockets have improved over

the years. At one time, these weapons were used against jeeps and other light vehicles. However, over the years their threat to tanks grew as their firepower grew.

A new type of rocket launcher ammunition was developed that could punch through the outer armor of the tank. A second explosion would then go off inside the tank. This type of ammunition shell was called the chemical energy round. Its success forced tank designers to invent stronger armor.

Specially designed armor was developed to deal with this problem. This armor was developed secretly in Great Britain. The armor was made of several layers of metal, with spaces between the layers. This allowed the armor to cushion the impact of the chemical energy rocket so that the second explosion would not harm the tank's crew. This type of armor is called Chobham armor.

Armor-piercing shells are used by the Abrams M1A1. They are deadly weapons against other tanks.

CHEMICAL AND BIOLOGICAL WEAPONS

The Abrams has special filters that clean the air drawn from the outside. These filters protect the tank crew from chemical and biological weapons. They also shield the inside of the Abrams from radioactivity. This NBC (Nuclear, Biological, Chemical) protection is used on the Soviet T-72 tank as well.

CHAPTER 4

TANK BATTLE AND THE ABRAMS'S DOMINANCE

When Leonardo da Vinci designed the first tank in the 1500s, he wanted to protect soldiers from arrows and spears as they marched toward the enemy. His design was a wagon with heavy armor attached. Such vehicles appeared from da Vinci's time onward. Their success depended on what kinds of weapons an enemy used. Rifle bullets bounced off steel armor. However, cannonballs smashed through this same steel armor.

Armored vehicles are easily protected against rifle bullets.

The tanks' success also depended on the slope of hills and valleys. If there were no roads, an armored vehicle could not move well over rocky or muddy ground. Armies began building better and better armored vehicles as time passed.

By the time World War I started, weapons and tactics differed from those of past wars. The armies faced each other across muddy fields with long trenches dug between them. No car or truck with regular wheels could drive across these fields. The trenches were too deep and the mud too thick. Heavy armored vehicles were needed to protect soldiers from machine gun fire. However, generals were afraid that armored vehicles would sink in the mud.

A British officer, Lt. Colonel Ernest Swinton, came up with the idea to solve army movement problems. Long metal tracks were connected around the wheels of the armored

The "caterpillar" tracks used on tanks and other armored vehicles help them travel through mud.

vehicles. These tracks had been used on farm tractors in the United States. The tracks were given the name caterpillar tracks. When linked together, the tracks moved in much the same way as a caterpillar moves its body as it crawls up and over everything in its path.

The tracks supported the heavy vehicles in the muddy fields. The tracks' length allowed the vehicles to cross the deep trenches without falling into them. The construction of

WWI tanks were built long and low so they could
travel over the deep trenches used in battle.

these first armored vehicles was top secret.
Even the workers who built them weren't told
how the vehicles were going to be used. The
workers thought they were building large
water containers for the desert. They called
them "tanks." This name stuck, even after the
true purpose of the vehicles became known.

The tanks proved successful in crossing the battlefield trenches. They were first used in the Battle of Somme on September 15, 1916. When the German soldiers saw these "armored giants" moving toward them, they panicked and ran. The tanks broke through enemy lines. The importance of the tank in battle now was known.

By the time World War II began, most countries had built their own tanks. Germany had designed a tank that was powerful and fast. They called it the Panzer, after the German word for armor. The panzer had 8-

Did you know?

There was a reason why American-made tanks used thin armor in WWII. All of America's tanks had to be shipped to Europe. This meant that each tank could not be too heavy. Otherwise, fewer tanks could be loaded onto cargo ships. However, their quickness helped these light-armored tanks to survive longer.

millimeter machine guns on its turret. Its cannon shot 88-millimeter shells.

The Germans also came up with tactics for how to use their tanks in battle. They used tanks to move quickly across the countryside. This quick advance surprised the enemy. Tank warfare had changed from one of defense to a powerful offense. Tanks became the weapon that drove through the country-side and blasted through towns. The rest of the soldiers followed behind the tanks to take the enemy's territory. The Germans called this tactic Blitzkrieg, which means "lightning strike."

THE FIGHT TO BE CALLED "THE BEST TANK IN THE WORLD"

At the start of the Gulf War, many military experts feared that the M1A1 Abrams tank would not run well in the Middle Eastern desert. The Abrams's turbine engine needed

Tanks can support a battle group
or lead a battle group.

clean air to run properly. The desert sand
might harm the engine. Also, the Iraqi army
was very large and well-armed. Iraq had five
thousand Soviet-made tanks. All of the Iraqi
tanks had been fitted with the latest guns to
make them even more powerful. The Soviet
T-72 tanks also had performed well in Iraq's
previous desert wars.

During the Gulf War (1991), not a single
Abrams tank was lost during battle.

On February 24, 1991, the ground war
began. American forces used special plows
attached to the front of the Abrams tank to
break through the Iraqi lines. Then other
Abrams tanks followed. The turbine engine
performed well in the sandy desert. Few

Abrams tanks broke down during the advance. The Abrams was the fastest-moving tank on the battlefield. The quiet and quick turbine engine allowed the Abrams to find and destroy the slower T-72 Soviet tanks. The thermal imaging system allowed the tank driver to see where he was going at night. This system also proved useful in the daytime because it helped the driver to see in the dusty, smoky conditions of the desert battlefield.

This was the largest armored battle in history. In just one hundred hours, more than 3,487 Iraqi tanks were destroyed or captured. No Abrams tanks were lost to enemy fire during the battle. The Iraqi soldiers began to give up fighting and surrender. The Gulf War was quickly won. The greater technology of American weapons helped the coalition forces to defeat the Iraqi army. The M1A1 Abrams tank helped to achieve this victory.

THE FUTURE OF THE ABRAMS TANK

After its outstanding performance in the Gulf War in 1991, the Abrams was regarded as the best tank in the world. The next generation of Abrams tanks, the M1A2 model, has many improvements. More depleted uranium armor is used, making the tank stronger. Computer improvements help the gunner and the tank commander both to choose targets and fire on them much more quickly. Communication between tanks also has improved. An under armor auxiliary power unit was developed to help charge the tank's batteries when the engine is not running. Future improvements in the Abrams's computer software will ensure that the M1A2 continues to be the best tank in the world, and of the future as well.

The M1A2 Abrams will have stronger armor and better electronic targeting and firing equipment.

105MM CANNON

MACHINE GUN

CREW MEMBERS

MACHINE GUN

TURRET

HEADLIGHT

CATERPILLAR TRACKS

GENERAL CHARACTERISTICS

MANUFACTURER: GENERAL DYNAMICS

WEIGHT: 63 TONS

LENGTH: 387 INCHES

WIDTH: 144 INCHES

WEAPONS: 3 MACHINE GUNS, 1 CANNON

MAXIMUM SPEED: 42 MPH

MAXIMUM DISTANCE: 275 MILES

CREW: FOUR

COST: $4,300,000

SIDE VIEW

TOP VIEW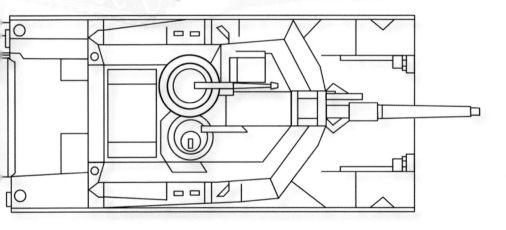

M1A1 LOADING ONTO A PLANE

NEW WORDS

Allies a group of twenty-six nations that fought against Germany, Italy, and Japan during World War II (1939–1945)

caterpillar track a connected steel track that rotates around a series of smaller wheels to allow the tank to travel over rough ground and trenches

chemical energy round rocket launcher ammunition round able to pierce the armor of a tank and then set off a second explosion inside the tank

Chobham armor armor designed with small spaces between the layers that protect against penetration by enemy shells

depleted uranium the heaviest of metals; depleted uranium is not radioactive.

detonate to explode

diesel a type of gasoline

laser rangefinder a device that shoots a laser beam of light at a target and shows the exact distance for the gunner's computer

periscope device that allows the crew to see outside from the inside of the tank

thermal imaging system device that shows the image of an enemy target, which is detected by the heat given off by that target

turbine a pressure-driven engine that works in a similar way to that of a jet plane

turret the rotating part of a tank that holds the guns and sits on top of the main body

Hogg, Ivan B. *Modern Military Techniques: Tanks.* Minneapolis, MN: Lerner Publications, 1985.

Kershaw, Andrew. *Explorer Guides: Tanks.* Windermere, FL: Ray Rourke Publishing, Inc., 1980.

Summers, Harry G., Jr. *The New Face of War: The Armored Fist.* Alexandria, VA: Time-Life Books, 1991.

Vann, Frank. *How They Work: M1A1 Abrams Main Battle Tank.* New York: Mallard Press, 1989.

RESOURCES

Web Sites

The Military Unit Database

http://geocities.com/pentagram/quarters/5227
This site gives detailed information about the Abrams tank. It includes pictures and specifications. It also contains information about military sea and air units.

The Tank Museum

www.tankmuseum.co.uk/collection.html
This online museum presents a sample of pictures from the museum's large collection of tanks. A variety of historical periods are covered. It includes experimental tanks and memorabilia.

RESOURCES

Organizations
U.S. Army
1500 Army Pentagon
Washington, D.C. 20310-1500
http://army.mil

INDEX

INDEX

About the Author

Michael A. Black is a veteran of the U.S. Army. He served in the early 1970s during the Vietnam War, and has always been interested in weapons and military history. His interests include reading, martial arts, and running. He is a police officer in the Chicago metropolitan area.